THE
BOATER'S LOG BOOK
& JOURNAL

whitecap

The information in this book is true and complete to the
best of our knowledge. All recommendations are made
without guarantee on the part of the author or Whitecap
Books. The author and publisher disclaim any liability
in connection with the use of this information. For
additional information, please contact Whitecap Books,
351 Lynn Avenue, North Vancouver, BC V7J 2C4.

Copy-editing and proofreading by Lisa Collins
Interior design by Jennifer Conroy
Cover design by Roberta Batchelor

Printed and bound in Canada.

Library and Archives Canada Cataloguing in Publication

The boater's log book & journal.

ISBN 1-55285-700-X

1. Boats and boating. 2. Diaries (Blank-books)
I. Title: Boater's log book and journal.
GV775.B62 2005   797.1   C2004-907079-7

The publisher acknowledges the support of the Canada
Council for the Arts and the Cultural Services Branch of
the Government of British Columbia for our publishing
program. We acknowledge the financial support of the
Government of Canada through the Book Industry
Development Program for publishing activities.

Contents

Introduction 7

Boat Basics 9

Before Setting Sail 10

Preparation Checklist 12

Cruising Log 17

Radio Log 113

Emergencies 123

Records and Notes 131

*I*ntroduction

Whether you're a novice or experienced boater, recording your voyages is both useful and exciting. An up-to-date log book can help you track equipment and fuel use, note well-equipped service providers, and, most importantly, keep a record of your adventures for the years to come.

Take the time to fill out each section of this log book. Even if recording the serial number of your new equipment doesn't seem important, you may need that information two years from now. Not only will the lists and charts provide a quick and easy reference tool for future maintenance, they are also an excellent guide for the next owner, if you ever choose to sell your vessel.

The Boater's Log Book and Journal is designed to be a personalized record, as well. Ample room for facts and information will allow you to adapt each page to your own needs. And room for notes will help you store memories of good experiences and bad—experiences that make each day on the water unique.

boat basics

General Information

Vessel Name

Type of Vessel   Home Port

I.D. Number   Radio Call Sign

Owner's Name

Address

Postal or Zip Code   Telephone

Emergency Contact

Important Registration or Licence Information

Builder/Manufacturer

Address

Postal or Zip Code   Telephone

Contact Name

Model	Year	Draft	Beam
Length (overall)	Length (on the water line)		Height
Displacement	Hull Material	Hull Color	Trim Color
Number of Masts	Mast Height(s)		

Propeller Size(s)   Rotation

Engine Make(s)   Engine Model(s)

Serial Number(s)   Oil Type(s)

Fuel Tank Capacity   Water Tank Capacity

Hot Water Tank Capacity   Generator Make

Generator Model   Transmission Make

Transmission Model   Transmission Oil

Insurer

Address

Postal or Zip Code   Telephone

Contact Name   Policy Number

Equipment

The following equipment is vital for your boating safety, and should be on board at all times. Check with boating authorities in your area for other equipment that may be required.

Powered Pleasure Craft (up to 6 meters/20 feet long)

➤ a personal flotation device or life jacket for each person on board
➤ a buoyant heaving line, at least 15 meters / 50 feet long
➤ an oar or paddle, or an anchor with at least 15 meters / 50 feet of rope, cable, or chain attached
➤ a fire extinguisher (Check with local authorities to determine which kind of extinguisher your boat requires.)
➤ a bailer or a manual water pump with hose
➤ a watertight flashlight or three flares
➤ a horn or other sound signaling device
➤ navigation lights

Pleasure Craft (6 to 8 meters/20 to 25 feet in length)

➤ a personal flotation device or life jacket for each person on board
➤ a buoyant heaving line, at least 15 meters / 50 feet long, or a life buoy attached to a buoyant line at least 15 meters / 50 feet long
➤ a ladder, or other reboarding device
➤ an oar or paddle, or an anchor with at least 15 meters / 50 feet of rope, cable, or chain attached
➤ one or two fire extinguishers (Check with local authorities to determine which kind of extinguisher your boat requires.)
➤ a bailer or a manual water pump with hose
➤ a watertight flashlight
➤ six flares
➤ a horn or other sound signaling device
➤ navigation lights

Pleasure Craft (8 to 12 meters/25 to 40 feet in length)

➤ a personal flotation device or life jacket for each person on board
➤ a buoyant heaving line, at least 15 meters / 50 feet long
➤ a life buoy, attached to a buoyant line at least 15 meters / 50 feet long
➤ a ladder or other reboarding device
➤ an anchor with at least 30 meters / 100 feet of rope, cable, or chain attached
➤ one or two fire extinguishers (Check with local authorities to determine which kind of extinguisher your boat requires.)
➤ a bailer
➤ a manual water pump with hose
➤ a watertight flashlight
➤ twelve flares
➤ a horn or other sound signaling device
➤ navigation lights

Pleasure Craft (12 to 20 meters/40 to 65 feet long)

➤ a personal flotation device or life jacket for each person on board
➤ a buoyant heaving line, at least 15 meters / 50 feet long
➤ a life buoy, attached to a buoyant line at least 15 meters / 50 feet long
➤ a ladder or other reboarding device
➤ an anchor with at least 50 meters / 170 feet of rope, cable, or chain attached
➤ bilge pumping arrangements
➤ a fire extinguisher at the entrance to any space with cooking, heating, or refrigerating appliances, at the entrance to any accommodation spaces, and at the entrance to the engine room (Check with local authorities to determine which kind of extinguishers your boat requires.)
➤ an axe
➤ two large buckets
➤ a watertight flashlight
➤ twelve flares
➤ two sound signaling devices (bell and whistle)
➤ navigation lights

preparation checklist

Use these pages to jot down chores to be done before embarking. Each time you set off on a journey, run quickly through your list to ensure all preparations are complete.

Crew Members and Duties
What needs to be accomplished before, during, and after your voyage? You can use these pages to list chores and the people responsible for each.

Before Departure
Chore   Crew Member

1. _____

2. _____

3. _____

4. _____

5. _____

6. _____

7. _____

8. _____

9. _____

10. _____

11. _____

12. _____

13. _____

14. _____

15. _____

There are several ways to signal distress:
➤ fly the code flag N (no) above the code flag C (yes)
➤ continuously sound your horn
➤ fire a flare, or, during the day, an orange smoke signal
➤ stretch both arms out to your sides and raise and lower them repeatedly

During the Voyage

Chore	Crew Member
1.	
2.	
3.	
4.	
5.	
6.	
7.	
8.	
9.	
10.	
11.	
12.	
13.	
14.	
15.	

Preparation Checklist

The Coast Guard recommends reviewing the following checklist before you set sail:

➤ What is the weather forecast?

➤ Any local hazards or boating restrictions?

➤ Do you have the necessary maps or charts?

➤ Are there life jackets or personal flotation devices for everyone on board?

➤ Is all safety equipment in good working order?

➤ Do you have ample reserves of fuel for the trip or will you need to refuel?

➤ Is your VHF radio working properly?

➤ Do you have a first-aid kit, basic tools, and spare parts on board?

➤ Have you told someone on shore where you are going, when you will be back, and what your boat looks like?

Upon Return

Chore   Crew Member

1. _____

2. _____

3. _____

4. _____

5. _____

6. _____

7. _____

8. _____

9. _____

10. _____

11. _____

12. _____

13. _____

14. _____

15. _____

"I am a student of those early explorers, and I never fail to be amazed and impressed by the tremendous courage that it must have taken to sail in those vast Arctic reaches, never knowing where they were going, and when they got there they didn't know where they were! And, of course, like Christopher Columbus, when they got back they had no idea where they had been or what they had discovered."

—Stuart M. Hodgson, NWT Commissioner

In Case of Emergency

Chore   Crew Member

1. _____

2. _____

3. _____

4. _____

5. _____

6. _____

7. _____

8. _____

9. _____

10. _____

11. _____

12. _____

13. _____

14. _____

15. _____

The Boater's Toolbox

Do you have the tools on board to deal with minor repairs?
Here are some things you may want to keep handy:

➤ Drive belts for your alternator and generator
➤ An assortment of fuses
➤ Extra light bulbs
➤ Solder
➤ Electrical and duct tape
➤ Grease for battery terminals

cruising log

Date

Departure Point

Arrival Point

Start Time   End Time

Forecast

Weather

Wind   Visibility

Distance Traveled

Average Speed

Engine (Average RPMs)

Fuel on Board

Notes & Remarks

cruising log

Date

Departure Point

Arrival Point

Start Time   End Time

Forecast

Weather

Wind   Visibility

Distance Traveled

Average Speed

Engine (Average RPMs)

Fuel on Board

Notes & Remarks

cruising log

Date

Departure Point

Arrival Point

Start Time   End Time

Forecast

Weather

Wind   Visibility

Distance Traveled

Average Speed

Engine (Average RPMs)

Fuel on Board

Notes & Remarks

cruising log

Date

Departure Point

Arrival Point

Start Time   End Time

Forecast

Weather

Wind   Visibility

Distance Traveled

Average Speed

Engine (Average RPMs)

Fuel on Board

Notes & Remarks

cruising log

Date

Departure Point

Arrival Point

Start Time   End Time

Forecast

Weather

Wind   Visibility

Distance Traveled

Average Speed

Engine (Average RPMs)

Fuel on Board

*"To be a good fisherman,
you have to be able
to think like a fish."*

—Edith Iglauer, essayist

Notes & Remarks

cruising log

Date

Departure Point

Arrival Point

Start Time   End Time

Forecast

Weather

Wind   Visibility

Distance Traveled

Average Speed

Engine (Average RPMs)

Fuel on Board

Notes & Remarks

cruising log

Date

Departure Point

Arrival Point

Start Time   End Time

Forecast

Weather

Wind   Visibility

Distance Traveled

Average Speed

Engine (Average RPMs)

Fuel on Board

Notes & Remarks

cruising log

Date

Departure Point

Arrival Point

Start Time   End Time

Forecast

Weather

Wind   Visibility

Distance Traveled

Average Speed

Engine (Average RPMs)

Fuel on Board

Notes & Remarks

cruising log

Date

Departure Point

Arrival Point

Start Time   End Time

Forecast

Weather

Wind   Visibility

Distance Traveled

Average Speed

Engine (Average RPMs)

Fuel on Board

Notes & Remarks

cruising log

Date

Departure Point

Arrival Point

Start Time   End Time

Forecast

Weather

Wind   Visibility

Distance Traveled

Average Speed

Engine (Average RPMs)

Fuel on Board

Notes & Remarks

cruising log

Date _____

Departure Point _____

Arrival Point _____

Start Time _____ End Time _____

Forecast _____

Weather _____

Wind _____ Visibility _____

Distance Traveled _____

Average Speed _____

Engine (Average RPMs) _____

Fuel on Board _____

Magnet Alert

Sound-system speakers contain magnets.
Avoid placing them near your compass,
or you will get false readings.

Notes & Remarks

_____

_____

_____

_____

_____

_____

_____

_____

_____

_____

_____

_____

_____

_____

cruising log

Date

Departure Point

Arrival Point

Start Time   End Time

Forecast

Weather

Wind   Visibility

Distance Traveled

Average Speed

Engine (Average RPMs)

Fuel on Board

Notes & Remarks

cruising log

Date

Departure Point

Arrival Point

Start Time   End Time

Forecast

Weather

Wind   Visibility

Distance Traveled

Average Speed

Engine (Average RPMs)

Fuel on Board

Notes & Remarks

cruising log

Date

Departure Point

Arrival Point

Start Time   End Time

Forecast

Weather

Wind   Visibility

Distance Traveled

Average Speed

Engine (Average RPMs)

Fuel on Board

Notes & Remarks

cruising log

Date

Departure Point

Arrival Point

Start Time   End Time

Forecast

Weather

Wind   Visibility

Distance Traveled

Average Speed

Engine (Average RPMs)

Fuel on Board

Notes & Remarks

cruising log

Date

Departure Point

Arrival Point

Start Time   End Time

Forecast

Weather

Wind   Visibility

Distance Traveled

Average Speed

Engine (Average RPMs)

Fuel on Board

Notes & Remarks

cruising log

Date

Departure Point

Arrival Point

Start Time   End Time

Forecast

Weather

Wind   Visibility

Distance Traveled

Average Speed

Engine (Average RPMs)

Fuel on Board

"The features of big lake travel—the vast-ness, the few constraints in finding shelter or campsites, and above all the potential peril from the power of big waves and high winds—are guarantees of its solitude."

—Eric W. Morse, historian

Notes & Remarks

cruising log

Date

Departure Point

Arrival Point

Start Time   End Time

Forecast

Weather

Wind   Visibility

Distance Traveled

Average Speed

Engine (Average RPMs)

Fuel on Board

Notes & Remarks

cruising log

Date

Departure Point

Arrival Point

Start Time   End Time

Forecast

Weather

Wind   Visibility

Distance Traveled

Average Speed

Engine (Average RPMs)

Fuel on Board

Notes & Remarks

cruising log

Date _____

Departure Point _____

Arrival Point _____

Start Time _____ End Time _____

Forecast _____

Weather _____

Wind _____ Visibility _____

Distance Traveled _____

Average Speed _____

Engine (Average RPMs) _____

Fuel on Board _____

Notes & Remarks _____

_____

_____

_____

_____

_____

_____

_____

_____

_____

_____

_____

_____

_____

cruising log

Date

Departure Point

Arrival Point

Start Time   End Time

Forecast

Weather

Wind   Visibility

Distance Traveled

Average Speed

Engine (Average RPMs)

Fuel on Board

Notes & Remarks

cruising log

Date

Departure Point

Arrival Point

Start Time   End Time

Forecast

Weather

Wind   Visibility

Distance Traveled

Average Speed

Engine (Average RPMs)

Fuel on Board

Notes & Remarks

cruising log

Date

Departure Point

Arrival Point

Start Time   End Time

Forecast

Weather

Wind   Visibility

Distance Traveled

Average Speed

Engine (Average RPMs)

Fuel on Board

Radio Safety

Have a qualified technician check
your radio every six months. This
may be the most important piece
of safety equipment on board.

Notes & Remarks

cruising log

Date

Departure Point

Arrival Point

Start Time   End Time

Forecast

Weather

Wind   Visibility

Distance Traveled

Average Speed

Engine (Average RPMs)

Fuel on Board

Notes & Remarks

cruising log

Date

Departure Point

Arrival Point

Start Time   End Time

Forecast

Weather

Wind   Visibility

Distance Traveled

Average Speed

Engine (Average RPMs)

Fuel on Board

Notes & Remarks

cruising log

Date

Departure Point

Arrival Point

Start Time   End Time

Forecast

Weather

Wind   Visibility

Distance Traveled

Average Speed

Engine (Average RPMs)

Fuel on Board

Notes & Remarks

cruising log

Date

Departure Point

Arrival Point

Start Time   End Time

Forecast

Weather

Wind   Visibility

Distance Traveled

Average Speed

Engine (Average RPMs)

Fuel on Board

Notes & Remarks

cruising log

Date

Departure Point

Arrival Point

Start Time   End Time

Forecast

Weather

Wind   Visibility

Distance Traveled

Average Speed

Engine (Average RPMs)

Fuel on Board

Notes & Remarks

cruising log

Date

Departure Point

Arrival Point

Start Time   End Time

Forecast

Weather

Wind   Visibility

Distance Traveled

Average Speed

Engine (Average RPMs)

Fuel on Board

*"The voice of the sea
speaks to the soul."*

—Kate Chopin, *The Awakening*

Notes & Remarks

cruising log

Date

Departure Point

Arrival Point

Start Time   End Time

Forecast

Weather

Wind   Visibility

Distance Traveled

Average Speed

Engine (Average RPMs)

Fuel on Board

Notes & Remarks

cruising log

Date

Departure Point

Arrival Point

Start Time   End Time

Forecast

Weather

Wind   Visibility

Distance Traveled

Average Speed

Engine (Average RPMs)

Fuel on Board

Notes & Remarks

cruising log

Date

Departure Point

Arrival Point

Start Time   End Time

Forecast

Weather

Wind   Visibility

Distance Traveled

Average Speed

Engine (Average RPMs)

Fuel on Board

Notes & Remarks

cruising log

Date

Departure Point

Arrival Point

Start Time   End Time

Forecast

Weather

Wind   Visibility

Distance Traveled

Average Speed

Engine (Average RPMs)

Fuel on Board

Notes & Remarks

cruising log

Date

Departure Point

Arrival Point

Start Time   End Time

Forecast

Weather

Wind   Visibility

Distance Traveled

Average Speed

Engine (Average RPMs)

Fuel on Board

Notes & Remarks

cruising log

Date

Departure Point

Arrival Point

Start Time   End Time

Forecast

Weather

Wind   Visibility

Distance Traveled

Average Speed

Engine (Average RPMs)

Fuel on Board

Tie It All Together!

Imagine your boat turned on its side. Does everything stay in place? Do the cupboards stay closed, and do heavy objects such as batteries slide around? Moving objects may harm your passengers or your vessel in rough water.

Notes & Remarks

cruising log

Date

Departure Point

Arrival Point

Start Time   End Time

Forecast

Weather

Wind   Visibility

Distance Traveled

Average Speed

Engine (Average RPMs)

Fuel on Board

Notes & Remarks

cruising log

Date

Departure Point

Arrival Point

Start Time   End Time

Forecast

Weather

Wind   Visibility

Distance Traveled

Average Speed

Engine (Average RPMs)

Fuel on Board

Notes & Remarks

cruising log

Date

Departure Point

Arrival Point

Start Time   End Time

Forecast

Weather

Wind   Visibility

Distance Traveled

Average Speed

Engine (Average RPMs)

Fuel on Board

Notes & Remarks

cruising log

Date

Departure Point

Arrival Point

Start Time   End Time

Forecast

Weather

Wind   Visibility

Distance Traveled

Average Speed

Engine (Average RPMs)

Fuel on Board

Notes & Remarks

cruising log

Date

Departure Point

Arrival Point

Start Time   End Time

Forecast

Weather

Wind   Visibility

Distance Traveled

Average Speed

Engine (Average RPMs)

Fuel on Board

Notes & Remarks

cruising log

Date

Departure Point

Arrival Point

Start Time   End Time

Forecast

Weather

Wind   Visibility

Distance Traveled

Average Speed

Engine (Average RPMs)

Fuel on Board

*"A river seems a magic thing.
A magic, moving, living part
of the earth itself."*

—Laura Gilpin, *The Rio Grande*

Notes & Remarks

cruising log

Date

Departure Point

Arrival Point

Start Time   End Time

Forecast

Weather

Wind   Visibility

Distance Traveled

Average Speed

Engine (Average RPMs)

Fuel on Board

Notes & Remarks

cruising log

Date

Departure Point

Arrival Point

Start Time   End Time

Forecast

Weather

Wind   Visibility

Distance Traveled

Average Speed

Engine (Average RPMs)

Fuel on Board

Notes & Remarks

cruising log

Date

Departure Point

Arrival Point

Start Time   End Time

Forecast

Weather

Wind   Visibility

Distance Traveled

Average Speed

Engine (Average RPMs)

Fuel on Board

Notes & Remarks

cruising log

Date _____

Departure Point _____

Arrival Point _____

Start Time _____ End Time _____

Forecast _____

Weather _____

Wind _____ Visibility _____

Distance Traveled _____

Average Speed _____

Engine (Average RPMs) _____

Fuel on Board _____

Notes & Remarks _____

_____

_____

_____

_____

_____

_____

_____

_____

_____

_____

_____

_____

cruising log

Date

Departure Point

Arrival Point

Start Time   End Time

Forecast

Weather

Wind   Visibility

Distance Traveled

Average Speed

Engine (Average RPMs)

Fuel on Board

Notes & Remarks

cruising log

Date

Departure Point

Arrival Point

Start Time   End Time

Forecast

Weather

Wind   Visibility

Distance Traveled

Average Speed

Engine (Average RPMs)

Fuel on Board

Common Sense Safety

Make sure your fire extinguisher is readily accessible. It is not necessarily best to store it where fire is likely to break out. You don't want to walk through a smoke-filled galley, for example, to access the extinguisher.

Notes & Remarks

cruising log

Date

Departure Point

Arrival Point

Start Time   End Time

Forecast

Weather

Wind   Visibility

Distance Traveled

Average Speed

Engine (Average RPMs)

Fuel on Board

Notes & Remarks

cruising log

Date

Departure Point

Arrival Point

Start Time   End Time

Forecast

Weather

Wind   Visibility

Distance Traveled

Average Speed

Engine (Average RPMs)

Fuel on Board

Notes & Remarks

cruising log

Date

Departure Point

Arrival Point

Start Time   End Time

Forecast

Weather

Wind   Visibility

Distance Traveled

Average Speed

Engine (Average RPMs)

Fuel on Board

Notes & Remarks

cruising log

Date

Departure Point

Arrival Point

Start Time   End Time

Forecast

Weather

Wind   Visibility

Distance Traveled

Average Speed

Engine (Average RPMs)

Fuel on Board

Notes & Remarks

cruising log

Date _____

Departure Point _____

Arrival Point _____

Start Time _____ End Time _____

Forecast _____

Weather _____

Wind _____ Visibility _____

Distance Traveled _____

Average Speed _____

Engine (Average RPMs) _____

Fuel on Board _____

Notes & Remarks _____

_____

_____

_____

_____

_____

_____

_____

_____

_____

_____

_____

_____

_____

_____

cruising log

Date

Departure Point

Arrival Point

Start Time   End Time

Forecast

Weather

Wind   Visibility

Distance Traveled

Average Speed

Engine (Average RPMs)

Fuel on Board

O God, thy sea is so great,
and my boat so small.

—Breton fishermen's prayer

Notes & Remarks

cruising log

Date

Departure Point

Arrival Point

Start Time   End Time

Forecast

Weather

Wind   Visibility

Distance Traveled

Average Speed

Engine (Average RPMs)

Fuel on Board

Notes & Remarks

cruising log

Date

Departure Point

Arrival Point

Start Time   End Time

Forecast

Weather

Wind   Visibility

Distance Traveled

Average Speed

Engine (Average RPMs)

Fuel on Board

Notes & Remarks

cruising log

Date

Departure Point

Arrival Point

Start Time   End Time

Forecast

Weather

Wind   Visibility

Distance Traveled

Average Speed

Engine (Average RPMs)

Fuel on Board

Notes & Remarks

cruising log

Date

Departure Point

Arrival Point

Start Time   End Time

Forecast

Weather

Wind   Visibility

Distance Traveled

Average Speed

Engine (Average RPMs)

Fuel on Board

Notes & Remarks

cruising log

Date

Departure Point

Arrival Point

Start Time   End Time

Forecast

Weather

Wind   Visibility

Distance Traveled

Average Speed

Engine (Average RPMs)

Fuel on Board

Notes & Remarks

cruising log

Date

Departure Point

Arrival Point

Start Time   End Time

Forecast

Weather

Wind   Visibility

Distance Traveled

Average Speed

Engine (Average RPMs)

Fuel on Board

Follow-the-Leader

Imagine that another navigator
is following your course, using
only your log book as a guide.
This will help you decide how
many details to include.

Notes & Remarks

cruising log

Date

Departure Point

Arrival Point

Start Time   End Time

Forecast

Weather

Wind   Visibility

Distance Traveled

Average Speed

Engine (Average RPMs)

Fuel on Board

Notes & Remarks

cruising log

Date

Departure Point

Arrival Point

Start Time   End Time

Forecast

Weather

Wind   Visibility

Distance Traveled

Average Speed

Engine (Average RPMs)

Fuel on Board

Notes & Remarks

cruising log

Date _____

Departure Point _____

Arrival Point _____

Start Time _____ End Time _____

Forecast _____

Weather _____

Wind _____ Visibility _____

Distance Traveled _____

Average Speed _____

Engine (Average RPMs) _____

Fuel on Board _____

Notes & Remarks _____

_____

_____

_____

_____

_____

_____

_____

_____

_____

_____

_____

_____

_____

cruising log

Date

Departure Point

Arrival Point

Start Time   End Time

Forecast

Weather

Wind   Visibility

Distance Traveled

Average Speed

Engine (Average RPMs)

Fuel on Board

Notes & Remarks

cruising log

Date

Departure Point

Arrival Point

Start Time   End Time

Forecast

Weather

Wind   Visibility

Distance Traveled

Average Speed

Engine (Average RPMs)

Fuel on Board

Notes & Remarks

cruising log

Date _____

Departure Point _____

Arrival Point _____

Start Time _____ End Time _____

Forecast _____

Weather _____

Wind _____ Visibility _____

Distance Traveled _____

Average Speed _____

Engine (Average RPMs) _____

Fuel on Board _____

"There is nothing—absolutely nothing—half so much worth doing as simply messing about in boats."

—Kenneth Grahame,
The Wind in the Willows

Notes & Remarks

_____

_____

_____

_____

_____

_____

_____

_____

_____

_____

_____

_____

_____

_____

cruising log

Date

Departure Point

Arrival Point

Start Time   End Time

Forecast

Weather

Wind   Visibility

Distance Traveled

Average Speed

Engine (Average RPMs)

Fuel on Board

Notes & Remarks

cruising log

Date

Departure Point

Arrival Point

Start Time   End Time

Forecast

Weather

Wind   Visibility

Distance Traveled

Average Speed

Engine (Average RPMs)

Fuel on Board

Notes & Remarks

cruising log

Date

Departure Point

Arrival Point

Start Time   End Time

Forecast

Weather

Wind   Visibility

Distance Traveled

Average Speed

Engine (Average RPMs)

Fuel on Board

Notes & Remarks

cruising log

Date _____

Departure Point _____

Arrival Point _____

Start Time _____ End Time _____

Forecast _____

Weather _____

Wind _____ Visibility _____

Distance Traveled _____

Average Speed _____

Engine (Average RPMs) _____

Fuel on Board _____

Notes & Remarks _____

_____

_____

_____

_____

_____

_____

_____

_____

_____

_____

_____

_____

_____

cruising log

Date

Departure Point

Arrival Point

Start Time   End Time

Forecast

Weather

Wind   Visibility

Distance Traveled

Average Speed

Engine (Average RPMs)

Fuel on Board

Notes & Remarks

cruising log

Date

Departure Point

Arrival Point

Start Time   End Time

Forecast

Weather

Wind   Visibility

Distance Traveled

Average Speed

Engine (Average RPMs)

Fuel on Board

Combing for Scraps

Demand for iron outpaced supply during the Second World War. Salvage ships combed the Atlantic coast for cannons, anchors, and other scrap metal from shipwrecks. In doing so, they drastically reduced the chances that archaeologists would ever be able to locate the wrecks.

Notes & Remarks

cruising log

Date

Departure Point

Arrival Point

Start Time   End Time

Forecast

Weather

Wind   Visibility

Distance Traveled

Average Speed

Engine (Average RPMs)

Fuel on Board

Notes & Remarks

cruising log

Date

Departure Point

Arrival Point

Start Time   End Time

Forecast

Weather

Wind   Visibility

Distance Traveled

Average Speed

Engine (Average RPMs)

Fuel on Board

Notes & Remarks

cruising log

Date

Departure Point

Arrival Point

Start Time   End Time

Forecast

Weather

Wind   Visibility

Distance Traveled

Average Speed

Engine (Average RPMs)

Fuel on Board

Notes & Remarks

cruising log

Date

Departure Point

Arrival Point

Start Time   End Time

Forecast

Weather

Wind   Visibility

Distance Traveled

Average Speed

Engine (Average RPMs)

Fuel on Board

Notes & Remarks

cruising log

Date _____

Departure Point _____

Arrival Point _____

Start Time _____ End Time _____

Forecast _____

Weather _____

Wind _____ Visibility _____

Distance Traveled _____

Average Speed _____

Engine (Average RPMs) _____

Fuel on Board _____

Notes & Remarks _____

_____

_____

_____

_____

_____

_____

_____

_____

_____

_____

_____

_____

_____

_____

cruising log

Date

Departure Point

Arrival Point

Start Time   End Time

Forecast

Weather

Wind   Visibility

Distance Traveled

Average Speed

Engine (Average RPMs)

Fuel on Board

"The larger the island of knowledge, the longer the shoreline of wonder."

—Joseph MacInnis, undersea explorer, remembering an old proverb

Notes & Remarks

cruising log

Date

Departure Point

Arrival Point

Start Time   End Time

Forecast

Weather

Wind   Visibility

Distance Traveled

Average Speed

Engine (Average RPMs)

Fuel on Board

Notes & Remarks

cruising log

Date

Departure Point

Arrival Point

Start Time   End Time

Forecast

Weather

Wind   Visibility

Distance Traveled

Average Speed

Engine (Average RPMs)

Fuel on Board

Notes & Remarks

cruising log

Date

Departure Point

Arrival Point

Start Time   End Time

Forecast

Weather

Wind   Visibility

Distance Traveled

Average Speed

Engine (Average RPMs)

Fuel on Board

Notes & Remarks

cruising log

Date

Departure Point

Arrival Point

Start Time   End Time

Forecast

Weather

Wind   Visibility

Distance Traveled

Average Speed

Engine (Average RPMs)

Fuel on Board

Notes & Remarks

cruising log

Date _____

Departure Point _____

Arrival Point _____

Start Time _____ End Time _____

Forecast _____

Weather _____

Wind _____ Visibility _____

Distance Traveled _____

Average Speed _____

Engine (Average RPMs) _____

Fuel on Board _____

Notes & Remarks _____

_____

_____

_____

_____

_____

_____

_____

_____

_____

_____

_____

_____

_____

cruising log

Date

Departure Point

Arrival Point

Start Time   End Time

Forecast

Weather

Wind   Visibility

Distance Traveled

Average Speed

Engine (Average RPMs)

Fuel on Board

The Lone Sailor

In 1895, Joshua Slocum was the first man to complete a solo circumnavigation of the globe. His adventures are recorded in the classic *Sailing Alone Around the World*.

Notes & Remarks

cruising log

Date _____

Departure Point _____

Arrival Point _____

Start Time _____ End Time _____

Forecast _____

Weather _____

Wind _____ Visibility _____

Distance Traveled _____

Average Speed _____

Engine (Average RPMs) _____

Fuel on Board _____

Notes & Remarks _____

_____

_____

_____

_____

_____

_____

_____

_____

_____

_____

_____

_____

_____

_____

cruising log

Date _____

Departure Point _____

Arrival Point _____

Start Time _____ End Time _____

Forecast _____

Weather _____

Wind _____ Visibility _____

Distance Traveled _____

Average Speed _____

Engine (Average RPMs) _____

Fuel on Board _____

Notes & Remarks

_____

_____

_____

_____

_____

_____

_____

_____

_____

_____

_____

_____

_____

cruising log

Date

Departure Point

Arrival Point

Start Time   End Time

Forecast

Weather

Wind   Visibility

Distance Traveled

Average Speed

Engine (Average RPMs)

Fuel on Board

Notes & Remarks

cruising log

Date

Departure Point

Arrival Point

Start Time   End Time

Forecast

Weather

Wind   Visibility

Distance Traveled

Average Speed

Engine (Average RPMs)

Fuel on Board

Notes & Remarks

cruising log

Date

Departure Point

Arrival Point

Start Time   End Time

Forecast

Weather

Wind   Visibility

Distance Traveled

Average Speed

Engine (Average RPMs)

Fuel on Board

Notes & Remarks

cruising log

Date

Departure Point

Arrival Point

Start Time   End Time

Forecast

Weather

Wind   Visibility

Distance Traveled

Average Speed

Engine (Average RPMs)

Fuel on Board

"It is the ship that stays afloat that gets to port."

—Sir Samuel Cunard, shipbuilder

Notes & Remarks

cruising log

Date

Departure Point

Arrival Point

Start Time   End Time

Forecast

Weather

Wind   Visibility

Distance Traveled

Average Speed

Engine (Average RPMs)

Fuel on Board

Notes & Remarks

cruising log

Date

Departure Point

Arrival Point

Start Time   End Time

Forecast

Weather

Wind   Visibility

Distance Traveled

Average Speed

Engine (Average RPMs)

Fuel on Board

Notes & Remarks

cruising log

Date

Departure Point

Arrival Point

Start Time   End Time

Forecast

Weather

Wind   Visibility

Distance Traveled

Average Speed

Engine (Average RPMs)

Fuel on Board

Notes & Remarks

cruising log

Date

Departure Point

Arrival Point

Start Time   End Time

Forecast

Weather

Wind   Visibility

Distance Traveled

Average Speed

Engine (Average RPMs)

Fuel on Board

Notes & Remarks

cruising log

Date

Departure Point

Arrival Point

Start Time   End Time

Forecast

Weather

Wind   Visibility

Distance Traveled

Average Speed

Engine (Average RPMs)

Fuel on Board

Notes & Remarks

cruising log

Date

Departure Point

Arrival Point

Start Time   End Time

Forecast

Weather

Wind   Visibility

Distance Traveled

Average Speed

Engine (Average RPMs)

Fuel on Board

A "Crazy" Race

Critics called the Singlehanded TransPac "crazy" when it was first held in 1978. The race runs 3402 kilometres (2,120 miles) from California to Hanalei Bay in Kauai. Skippers sail the entire length of the race alone.

Notes & Remarks

radio log

Vessel Name _____ Call Sign _____

Date	Time	Channel	Location	Notes
				Phonetic Alphabet
				Alfa
				Bravo
				Charlie
				Delta
				Echo
				Foxtrot
				Golf
				Hotel
				India
				Juliet
				Kilo
				Lima
				Mike
				November
				Oscar
				Papa
				Quebec
				Romeo
				Sierra
				Tango
				Uniform
				Victor
				Whiskey
				X-Ray
				Yankee
				Zulu

radio log

Vessel Name _____ Call Sign _____

Date	Time	Channel	Location	Notes	
					Phonetic Alphabet
					Alfa
					Bravo
					Charlie
					Delta
					Echo
					Foxtrot
					Golf
					Hotel
					India
					Juliet
					Kilo
					Lima
					Mike
					November
					Oscar
					Papa
					Quebec
					Romeo
					Sierra
					Tango
					Uniform
					Victor
					Whiskey
					X-Ray
					Yankee
					Zulu

radio log

Vessel Name _____   Call Sign _____

Date	Time	Channel	Location	Notes
				Phonetic Alphabet
				Alfa
				Bravo
				Charlie
				Delta
				Echo
				Foxtrot
				Golf
				Hotel
				India
				Juliet
				Kilo
				Lima
				Mike
				November
				Oscar
				Papa
				Quebec
				Romeo
				Sierra
				Tango
				Uniform
				Victor
				Whiskey
				X-Ray
				Yankee
				Zulu

radio log

Vessel Name _____ Call Sign _____

Date	Time	Channel	Location	Notes	
					Phonetic Alphabet
					Alfa
					Bravo
					Charlie
					Delta
					Echo
					Foxtrot
					Golf
					Hotel
					India
					Juliet
					Kilo
					Lima
					Mike
					November
					Oscar
					Papa
					Quebec
					Romeo
					Sierra
					Tango
					Uniform
					Victor
					Whiskey
					X-Ray
					Yankee
					Zulu

radio log

Vessel Name _____   Call Sign _____

Date	Time	Channel	Location	Notes
				Phonetic Alphabet
				Alfa
				Bravo
				Charlie
				Delta
				Echo
				Foxtrot
				Golf
				Hotel
				India
				Juliet
				Kilo
				Lima
				Mike
				November
				Oscar
				Papa
				Quebec
				Romeo
				Sierra
				Tango
				Uniform
				Victor
				Whiskey
				X-Ray
				Yankee
				Zulu

radio log

Vessel Name				Call Sign	

Date	Time	Channel	Location	Notes	
					Phonetic Alphabet
					Alfa
					Bravo
					Charlie
					Delta
					Echo
					Foxtrot
					Golf
					Hotel
					India
					Juliet
					Kilo
					Lima
					Mike
					November
					Oscar
					Papa
					Quebec
					Romeo
					Sierra
					Tango
					Uniform
					Victor
					Whiskey
					X-Ray
					Yankee
					Zulu

radio log

| Vessel Name | | | Call Sign | |

Date	Time	Channel	Location	Notes
				Phonetic Alphabet
				Alfa
				Bravo
				Charlie
				Delta
				Echo
				Foxtrot
				Golf
				Hotel
				India
				Juliet
				Kilo
				Lima
				Mike
				November
				Oscar
				Papa
				Quebec
				Romeo
				Sierra
				Tango
				Uniform
				Victor
				Whiskey
				X-Ray
				Yankee
				Zulu

radio log

Vessel Name _____ Call Sign _____

Date	Time	Channel	Location	Notes	
					Phonetic Alphabet
					Alfa
					Bravo
					Charlie
					Delta
					Echo
					Foxtrot
					Golf
					Hotel
					India
					Juliet
					Kilo
					Lima
					Mike
					November
					Oscar
					Papa
					Quebec
					Romeo
					Sierra
					Tango
					Uniform
					Victor
					Whiskey
					X-Ray
					Yankee
					Zulu

radio log

Vessel Name				Call Sign

Date	Time	Channel	Location	Notes
				Phonetic Alphabet
				Alfa
				Bravo
				Charlie
				Delta
				Echo
				Foxtrot
				Golf
				Hotel
				India
				Juliet
				Kilo
				Lima
				Mike
				November
				Oscar
				Papa
				Quebec
				Romeo
				Sierra
				Tango
				Uniform
				Victor
				Whiskey
				X-Ray
				Yankee
				Zulu

emergencies

Sending a MAYDAY Message

Send a MAYDAY message only when you, your crew, or your vessel is in immediate danger. You should keep a copy of these instructions in an easy-to-find position near the radio.

1. Select the emergency channel or frequency, and ensure the power is on high.
2. Repeat "MAYDAY" three times.
3. Repeat your radio call sign three times.
4. Repeat your vessel name three times.
5. Give your position, by latitude and longitude, or a bearing taken from landmarks on shore.
6. State the nature of your distress (medical emergency, fire, sinking, etc.)
7. State how many people are on board and whether they are injured.
8. If there is time, provide additional information, such as a description of your vessel.

In Case of Fire

List the fire extinguishers on your vessel, and ensure that everyone on board is familiar with the uses and locations of these extinguishers.

Extinguisher Type	Location	Uses

In Case of a Hull Breach

These are some of the steps you may wish to take:

1. Call for help if the breach is severe.
2. Turn on an electric pump or pumps.
3. Place a cushion or pillow over the hole, then a board over the cushion. This should reduce the amount of water coming into the boat.

On the following lines, list the procedures you will follow in case of a hull breach. Include the location of emergency feathering or patching supplies and any extra pumping or bailing equipment available.

_____

_____

_____

_____

_____

_____

_____

_____

_____

_____

_____

_____

Know Your Stuff

More than half of search and rescue operations involve recreational boats. About half the distress calls made by pleasure boaters are because of mechanical difficulties, including running out of fuel. Knowing your safety and maintenance procedures and properly training yourself and others on board can help you avoid unnecessary emergencies.

In Case of Man Overboard

Here are some steps you may wish to take:

1. Alert the crew by shouting "Man overboard."
2. Assign one person to keep his or her eyes only on the person in the water.
3. Throw a buoy or life preserver to the person in the water.
4. Return the boat to the victim, or draw the victim alongside using a line.
5. Help the victim reboard the boat.

On the following lines, list the procedures you will follow if a passenger falls overboard. Include the location of emergency equipment such as life preservers, buoys, buoyant lines, ladders, or slings.

_____

_____

_____

_____

_____

_____

_____

_____

_____

_____

Drinking on Board

If you're operating a boat while intoxicated, your reflexes will be slower, your movements will be less precise, and your judgment will be impaired. The effects of the sun, the movement of the boat, or fatigue can amplify these problems. In fact, at least 40 percent of boating fatalities involve the use of alcohol.

In Case of Injury

If you are unsure of how to treat an injured person, use your radio to ask for help or advice. The following information from St. John Ambulance will help you address some of the most common boating injuries.

Basic First Aid

Make sure you and your crew are aware of basic first-aid procedures. When you're on the water, there may be no one else to help. Take a first-aid course, learn CPR, and carry a first-aid kit. These are some of the first steps to basic safety.

Emergency Scene Management

In the event of a mishap, where do you start? To ensure that first aid for life-threatening conditions is given safely and in the proper order, a sequence of priorities has been developed. Although the circumstances may dictate that the order be changed, steps should usually be taken in the following order:

1. Take charge of the situation.
2. Call or signal to attract the attention of other boaters or bystanders to assist you.
3. Assess the hazards at the scene.
4. Determine the history, number of casualties, and mechanism of injury.
5. Make the area safe for yourself and others.
6. Identify yourself to the casualties as a First Aider and offer to help.
7. Quickly assess the casualties for life-threatening conditions.
8. Send someone to call for help.
9. Give first aid for life-threatening conditions.

Artificial Respiration

When breathing has stopped for any reason, begin mouth-to-mouth artificial respiration.

➤ Tilt the head back by pressing down on the forehead with one hand.
➤ Place the fingers of the other hand under the chin and lift upward to pull the jaw up and to lift the tongue away from the back of the throat. This will open the airway to allow air to reach the lungs.
➤ Take 3–5 seconds to assess breathing.
➤ If there is no breathing, pinch the casualty's nostrils between your thumb and forefinger.
➤ Take a deep breath, place your open mouth over the casualty's mouth, making a tight seal, and blow slowly into the mouth.
➤ Take your mouth away and let the casualty exhale.
➤ Give one more breath.
➤ Assess the carotid pulse for 5–10 seconds.
➤ If a pulse is present, resume artificial respiration, breathing for the adult casualty at a rate of one breath every 5 seconds.
➤ If there is no pulse, begin CPR.

Bleeding

Most bleeding can be stopped by applying pressure on the wound by elevating the injured part, and by placing the casualty at rest. To control severe bleeding, apply hand pressure over a clean cloth if available. If the dressing becomes blood soaked, do not remove it. Place another dressing over the first. Lie the person down. Do not remove any foreign object embedded in the wound. Loosely cover the object with a light dressing to prevent further infection, then apply pressure around the object with a ring pad bandaged in place.

Unconsciousness

Unconsciousness can be caused by many conditions such as a blow to the head, shock, stroke, or diabetes. If the person is not breathing, begin mouth-to-mouth artificial respiration immediately. Control severe bleeding if present.

If injuries permit, place the person in the recovery position. Give nothing by mouth and keep the person warm. Anyone who has been unconscious should be seen by a physician.

Burns

Lessen the spread of heat in the tissues and relieve pain by immediately immersing the burned area in cold water or applying cloths soaked in water. Don't place a burn under extreme water pressure, like a strong-running tap, as this may further damage the tissue. Do not apply butter, ointments, or oil dressings. Cover the area with a clean cloth. If the burn is more severe and the skin is broken, simply cover with a clean cloth and seek immediate medical attention. If there is danger of swelling or blisters forming, remove rings or other jewelry and constrictive clothing, which may interfere with later treatment.

Sunburn

For minor sunburn, get into the shade and apply cool water or cloths soaked in cool water to relieve pain. Reaction to extreme exposure may be swelling and blistering. These cases should be treated as severe burns and covered with clean, dry dressings to prevent infection. Medical aid should be obtained. In the case of swelling or blisters forming, remove rings or other jewelry and constrictive clothing, which may interfere with later treatment.

Heat Exhaustion

Caused by exposure to excessive heat, especially moist heat, heat exhaustion is often accompanied by nausea and vomiting. Some of the following signs and symptoms may be present: muscular cramps, headache, dizziness, exhaustion, pale skin, weak pulse, rapid and shallow breathing, and cold, clammy skin. Place the person at rest in a cool place and give her/him water, as much as the casualty will drink. If the person is unconscious, do not give anything by mouth. Place the unconscious person in the recovery position and get immediate aid.

Heatstroke

A very serious illness, heatstroke is caused by exposure to high temperatures and hot, dry winds or high humidity and poor circulation. Symptoms are: a flushed face and hot, dry skin; temperature above 40°C/104°F; full, pounding pulse; noisy breathing; restlessness; headache; and dizziness. Unconsciousness may develop quickly and convulsions may occur. The casualty may die unless body temperature is reduced. To do so, remove the casualty's clothing and immerse the person in a cold bath, or wrap in a wet, cold sheet. Keep the sheet wet. If unconscious, place the casualty in the recovery position. When the body temperature is lowered to 38°C/100°F (slightly above normal), cover the casualty with a dry sheet and keep as cool as possible. Obtain medical aid immediately.

Hypothermia

Immersion in cold water or exposure to cool air in water-soaked clothing can lead to hypothermia. Shivering, slurred speech, stumbling, and drowsiness after exposure to cold are indications of hypothermia. The condition is severe when shivering stops. Unconsciousness and stopped breathing may follow. Move the casualty gently to shelter. Movement or rough handling can upset heart rhythm. Remove wet clothing and wrap in warm covers. Give warm, sweet drinks if the person is conscious and has mild hypothermia. Monitor breathing and give artificial respiration if needed. Obtain medical aid as soon as possible.

records & notes

Notes on Your Equipment

You may wish to record what emergency equipment, spare parts, and general supplies you have on board. Update this list regularly, so you can easily tell what you need to purchase on your next trip to the marina.

Equipment Item	Description	Serial Number	Location on Board

Notes on Your Equipment (continued)

Equipment Item	Description	Serial Number	Location on Board

Maintenance Log

This table will help you track equipment maintenance and the cost of repairs.

Date	Engine Hours	Location	Repair Type	Cost	Service Provider

Notes

Maintenance Log (continued)

Date	Engine Hours	Location	Repair Type	Cost	Service Provider

Notes

Maintenance Log (continued)

Date	Engine Hours	Location	Repair Type	Cost	Service Provider

Notes

Maintenance Log (continued)

Date	Engine Hours	Location	Repair Type	Cost	Service Provider

Notes

Fuel Log

Keeping a fuel log will help you track the amount and cost of fuel your vessel is using.

Date	Engine Hours	Cost per Liter/Gallon	Total Liters/Gallons	Total Cost	LPH/GPH

Notes

Fuel Log (continued)

Date	Engine Hours	Cost per Liter/Gallon	Total Liters/Gallons	Total Cost	LPH/GPH

Notes

Fuel Log (continued)

Date	Engine Hours	Cost per Liter/Gallon	Total Liters/Gallons	Total Cost	LPH/GPH

Notes

Fuel Log (continued)

Date	Engine Hours	Cost per Liter/Gallon	Total Liters/Gallons	Total Cost	LPH/GPH

Notes

Suppliers and Dealers

Use this area to record the names and contact information of suppliers you deal with regularly.

Name: _____
Address: _____
Postal or Zip Code: _____
Telephone: _____
Contact Name: _____
Specialty: _____

Name: _____
Address: _____
Postal or Zip Code: _____
Telephone: _____
Contact Name: _____
Specialty: _____

Name: _____
Address: _____
Postal or Zip Code: _____
Telephone: _____
Contact Name: _____
Specialty: _____

Name: _____
Address: _____
Postal or Zip Code: _____
Telephone: _____
Contact Name: _____
Specialty: _____

Name: _____
Address: _____
Postal or Zip Code: _____
Telephone: _____
Contact Name: _____
Specialty: _____

Name: _____
Address: _____
Postal or Zip Code: _____
Telephone: _____
Contact Name: _____
Specialty: _____

Recommended Suppliers

Use this area to record names and contact information for suppliers recommended by others.

Name: _____

Address: _____

Postal or Zip Code: _____

Telephone: _____

Contact Name: _____

Specialty: _____

Name: _____

Address: _____

Postal or Zip Code: _____

Telephone: _____

Contact Name: _____

Specialty: _____

Name: _____

Address: _____

Postal or Zip Code: _____

Telephone: _____

Contact Name: _____

Specialty: _____

Name: _____

Address: _____

Postal or Zip Code: _____

Telephone: _____

Contact Name: _____

Specialty: _____

Name: _____

Address: _____

Postal or Zip Code: _____

Telephone: _____

Contact Name: _____

Specialty: _____

Name: _____

Address: _____

Postal or Zip Code: _____

Telephone: _____

Contact Name: _____

Specialty: _____